This book belongs to

_____

"BOB DYLAN PLAY BOOK"
MATTEO GUARNACCIA

© ACC Art Books Ltd., 2016

World copyright reserved

ISBN 978-1-85149-821-5

Originally published in Italian by 24 ORE Cultura srl, Milan in 2015

English language translation by Sylvia Notini

British Library Cataloguing-in-Publication Data
A catalogue record for this book is available from the British Library

Printed and bound in China for ACC Editions,
an imprint of ACC Art Books Ltd., Woodbridge, Suffolk, UK

THIS BOOK IS A TRIBUTE TO THE AMERICAN POET (DULUTH, MINNESOTA, IN-THE-MIDDLE-OF-NOWHERE, 1941).
IT CONTAINS A SERIES OF EYE-CATCHING PICTURES THAT WILL LET THE READER PLAY AND HAVE FUN WHILE GOING OVER THE FIRST FABULOUS PERIOD IN BOB'S CAREER, FROM THE LATE 1950S TO JULY 1966, THE DATE OF THE MOTORCYCLE ACCIDENT SHROUDED IN MYSTERY THAT CAUSED HIM TO WITHDRAW TEMPORARILY FROM THE MUSIC SCENE.
IT WAS A SEASON OF ENLIGHTENMENT, UNBRIDLED CREATIVITY, WORKS OF GENIUS EXPRESSED THROUGH MUSIC, LYRICS, AND REVOLUTIONARY AESTHETIC INVENTIVENESS. THIS BOOK ALSO OFFERS YOU ONE OF THE COOLEST WARDROBES OF ALL TIME.
HAVE FUN!

M. G.

TABLE OF CONTENTS

YOUNG BOB, STILL A ZIMMERMAN, IN DULUTH

BOB'S TEENAGE OUTFIT

BOB'S ROCK 'N' ROLL HEROES

BOB'S FIRST GIRLFRIEND, ECHO HELSTROM

THE BLINKING BOB & HITCHHIKIN' BOB

HOBO OUTFIT AND BOB'S NEW INSPIRATIONS

BOB'S MUSE, SUZE ROTOLO

POETS, MUSICIANS, AND VISIONARIES

JOAN BAEZ & FRIENDS

GREENWICH VILLAGE CLUBS

BOB MEETS ALLEN GINSBERG, 1963

BOB TURNS THE BEATLES ON TO POT, 1964

BOB GOES ELECTRIC, 1965

FOLK-ROCK BOB, 1965

SUPERCOOL BOB, 1967

"PLAY IT FUCKIN' LOUD"

FRANÇOISE HARDY (OH-LA-LA!)

BOB DYLAN PARAPHERNALIA

SAD-EYED LADY SARA LOWNDS...

BOB DYLAN RACING BOARD GAME

BOB DYLAN CIRCUS, CHARACTERS, AND MAGIC BOX

BOB RIDING HIS TRIUMPH BONNEVILLE, 1966

Clothes Line Saga

by Giulia Pivetta

From a sociological point of view, Bob Dylan certainly played a pivotal role in the evolution of culture in the Sixties. It was a decade of profound change for Western civilization, and over a very short period of time, the political scene, the economy, culture, not to mention the existential sphere, all changed radically. With the advent of rampant consumerism, the struggle for civil rights, youth protests, the space race, and the introduction of the birth control pill, a collective transformation of historical bearing took place.

The practical side of this could be seen in everyday life. It could be perceived in the dramatic change in the values of the hearts and souls of the people, especially the younger generation. During the postwar boom, although the United States appeared to be the best of worlds to those looking at it from the outside, within the country itself the dominant white male model was being called into question by the new ideologies. In the stalemate that followed the decline of the WASP (White, Anglo-Saxon, Protestant), Bob Dylan was seen as a figure capable of offering guidance in an atmosphere of generalized insecurity.

Matteo Guarnaccia's encounter with art, which he has pushed beyond the limits imposed by methodology and tradition, offers us a new way of looking at Bob Dylan. An artist and illustrator who has chosen psychedelia as a medium, Guarnaccia was influenced more by rock music than by art school. As a member of the generation of young minds that absorbed in real time the release of albums like *Bringing It All Back Home*, *Highway 61 Revisited*, and *Blonde on Blonde*, Guarnaccia learned an important lesson from the music: that the meaning of everything lies in the smallest detail. From the Sixties onwards, album covers finally offered listeners insights into the world of the artist, a world that was now accessible to all. Bob Dylan's own album covers included cryptic messages, quotations, allusions to his cultural and personal world, creating a direct connection that reduced the distances between space and time to zero. This same continuous connection underlies Guarnaccia's approach to art, as well. The two artists have developed a way of telling their stories that is known as *stream of consciousness* in literary criticism – a necessity, not a method, that equates with freedom of thought for both of them.

Guarnaccia's free-flowing line well reflects Dylan's artistic and aesthetic evolution, via which he intercepts signals from the outside world and makes them his own. Over and over again Dylan has shown how he can metamorphose and take a new turn: from his debut as a rockabilly singer, borrowing his look from James Dean, to his hobo period, and to the electric revolution of 1965 and a psychedelic phase the following year, which ended with a motorcycle accident that marked a change in Dylan's outlook and his philosophy of life.

The art of moving unexpectedly across different languages and sounds has become the poet's distinctive feature, and this corresponds to the complete overturning of the social, geographic, and aesthetic references in force. Although he doesn't want to be identified as a spokesperson for the message of the Sixties, Dylan has still managed to enact its splendors and mysteries through his music and aesthetics, akin to a modern-day troubadour. This desire not to be caged inside a particular category is what encourages him to rework his style again and again. By breaking any habits he might be thought to have, he stresses the artist's right not to be labeled. With Dylan, the figure of the poet is offered a new identity, his music gives poetry a new name, imbuing rock 'n' roll with a high literary meaning.

The way people introduce themselves is through their appearance, using it as a calling card of sorts. In time, the more societies have become complex and fragmented, the more appearance has grown in importance. Only through visual language can one "speak" instantaneously, plainly, overcoming the barriers of verbal communication. Dylan understood the expressive potential of this means from the outset: beating Bowie to the draw, Dylan turned himself into an extension of the sound performance, enveloping the story by singing about specific emotional contexts. His Cuban-heeled boots and suede jacket on the cover of *Freewheelin'*, the houndstooth check suit he wore at the Royal Albert Hall in London, have become narrative elements, doors that open up to other dimensions through which to read a slice of twentieth-century history.

JANUARY 31, 1959

18-YEAR-OLD BOB TRAVELED FROM HIBBING TO DULUTH TO SEE BUDDY HOLLY & THE CRICKETS, RITCHIE VALENS, AND THE BIG BOPPER!!!

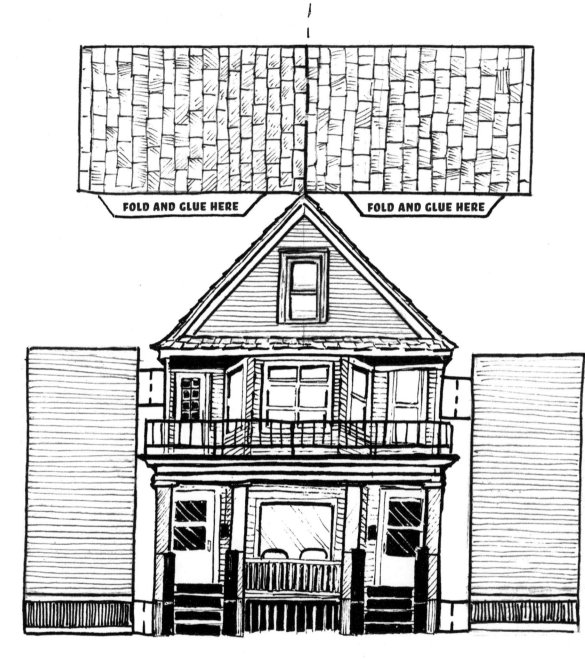

FOLD AND GLUE HERE   FOLD AND GLUE HERE

BOB'S BOYHOOD HOME IN DULUTH
519 N. 3RD AVENUE EAST

THE ZIMMERMAN FAMILY
LIVED ON THE TOP FLOOR

SOFT DENIM JEANS WITH ROLL-UP CUFFS

SIGN FOR THE ELECTRICAL APPLIANCE STORE WHERE BOB'S FATHER, ABRAM, WORKED.

THE HOME OF MICKA ELECTRIC CO.
GENERAL ELECTRIC APPLIANCES GE Maytag WASHERS

Mom & Dad

NO DOUBT ABOUT IT: BOB GETS HIS CURLY HAIR FROM MOM

STAGE JACKET

Little Richard
Buddy Holly
Bob Heroes

THE BLINKING BOB!

CARDBOARD MODEL THAT ACTUALLY WORKS TO ENTERTAIN YOUR FRIENDS

BACK

FINISHED MODEL

CUT OUT THE SLIT

CUT OUT THE EYES,

CUT OUT THE SLIT

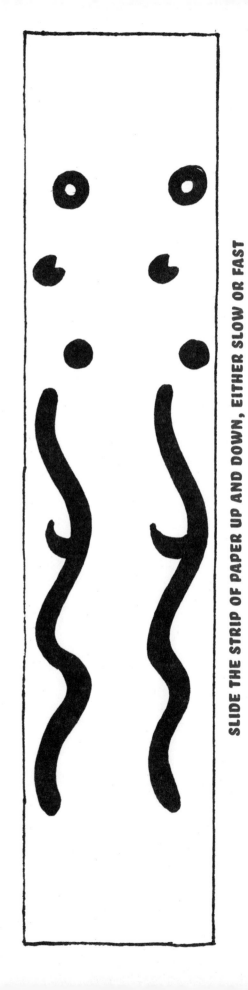

SLIDE THE STRIP OF PAPER UP AND DOWN, EITHER SLOW OR FAST

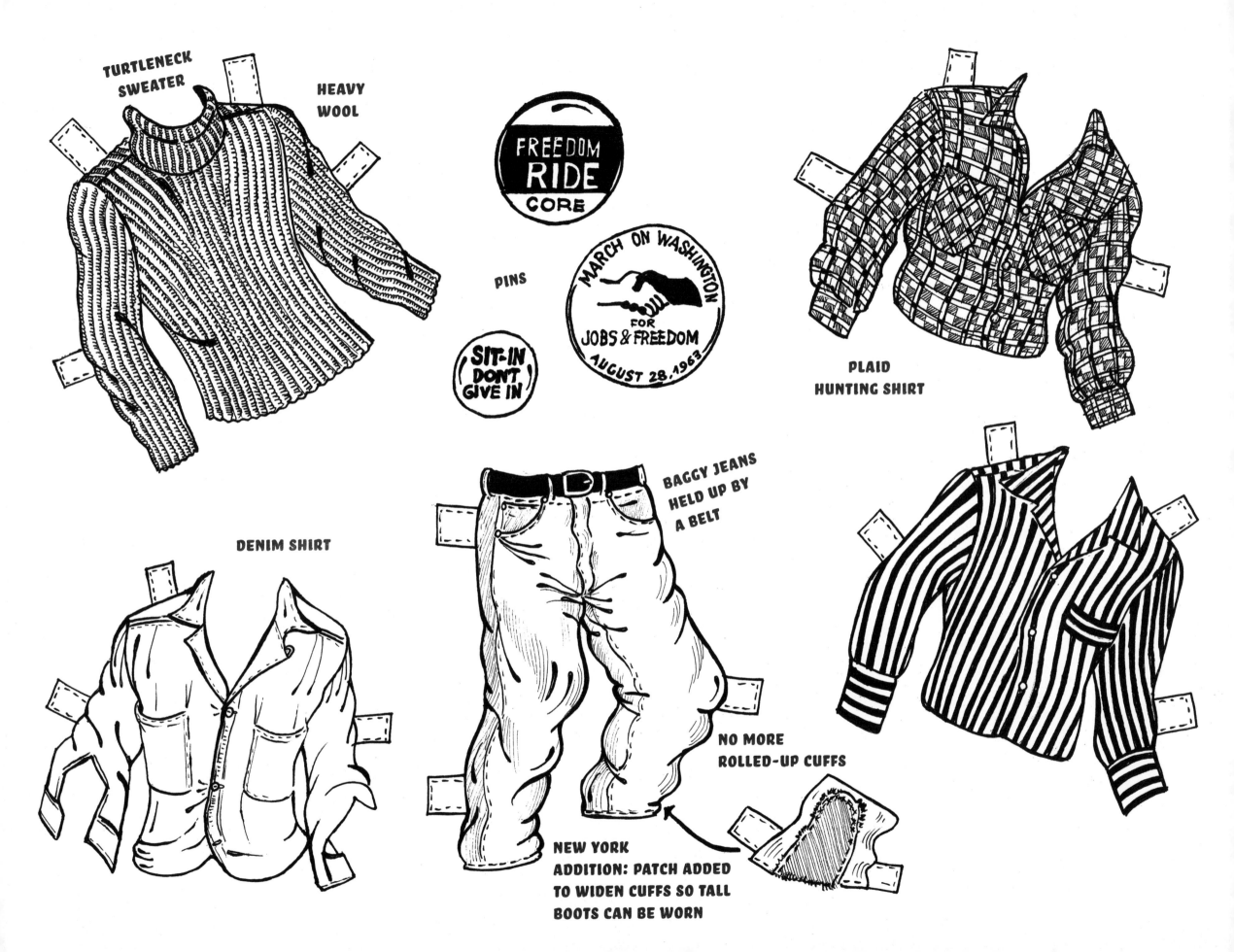

TURTLENECK SWEATER

HEAVY WOOL

FREEDOM RIDE CORE

PINS

SIT-IN DON'T GIVE IN

MARCH ON WASHINGTON FOR JOBS & FREEDOM AUGUST 28, 1963

PLAID HUNTING SHIRT

DENIM SHIRT

BAGGY JEANS HELD UP BY A BELT

NO MORE ROLLED-UP CUFFS

NEW YORK ADDITION: PATCH ADDED TO WIDEN CUFFS SO TALL BOOTS CAN BE WORN

GREETINGS from MINNEAPOLIS MINN.

Leadbelly

TELL ME BABY
BLACK WATER BLUES

ELLA SPEED
ON A CHRISTMAS
SWEET MARY BLUES
WESTERN PLAIN

HE'S REALLY INTO LEADBELLY'S BLUES!

SUEDE JACKET

MARINE BAND M. Hohner

SHEEPSKIN COAT

MINNESOTA
US
61

SIGN POST FOR HIGHWAY 61, FROM MINNESOTA TO LOUISIANA – BLUES H'WAY

BOB GIRLS! 2

The Muse

SUZE ROTOLO

THE GIRL IN "BOOTS OF SPANISH LEATHER"

ADVENTURES

JOY

LOVE

MYSTERIES

SECRETS

Bob Inspirational Band

Arthur Rimbaud
VISIONARY

Robert Burns
POET

Bertolt Brecht
POET, PLAYWRIGHT, AND
THEATER DIRECTOR

Woody Guthrie
FOLK MUSICIAN

Dylan Thomas
POET
(IN THE MIDDLE)

THIS MACHINE KILLS FASCISTS

JOAN BAEZ!

I HAD A DREAM

EQUALITY NOW!

FALLOUT SHELTER

BOB 3 GIRLS
COLLECT THEM ALL!!

★ The Protest Song Madonna! ★

SIT-IN DON'T GIVE IN

FREEDOM RIDE CORE

GREENWICH VILLAGE ~ BOB MAP

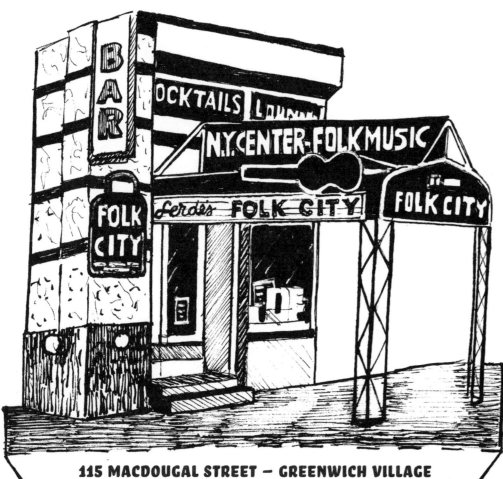

115 MACDOUGAL STREET – GREENWICH VILLAGE

Gerde's Folk City

THE HEART OF THE NY FOLK SCENE! A SLICE OF THE HISTORY OF AMERICAN POPULAR MUSIC

Cafe Wha?

THE JOINT WHERE BOB, JUST ARRIVED FROM NEW YORK (JANUARY 1961), WOULD SING 'TIL HE WAS HOARSE FOR A DOLLAR A DAY!

- OPEN EVERY NIGHT
- EATING AND DRINKING OPTIONAL
- MONDAYS HOOTENANNY & GUEST NIGHT
- FREE ADMISSION

11 WEST 4TH STREET - GREENWICH VILLAGE

Kettle of Fish

NEXT DOOR TO THE GASLIGHT CAFE, WHICH DIDN'T HAVE A LIQUOR LICENSE, THE KETTLE OF FISH HOSTED BEATNIKS, FOLKIES, AND A MEDLEY OF NIGHT CREATURES

Gaslight Cafe

IT WAS RIGHT AT THE BOTTOM OF THIS FLIGHT OF STAIRS THAT BOB SANG "MASTERS OF WAR" FOR THE FIRST TIME! (AND JACK KEROUAC READ HIS POETRY IN 1960)

Washington Square Arch, New York

THE NY FOLK SCENE WOULD MEET UP IN WASHINGTON SQUARE PARK, RIGHT IN FRONT OF THE TRIUMPHAL ARCH. EVERY SUNDAY YOU COULD SEE AND LISTEN TO THE FUTURE POP STARS, OR PEOPLE JUST PLONKING AWAY — FROM MARY TRAVERS (OF PETER, PAUL & MARY) TO BOB HIMSELF...

Cafe Figaro

ON THE CORNER OF MACDOUGAL AND BLEECKER STREETS

Let Bob play around the Village!

- CUT OUT THE FIGURES
- FOLD ALONG LINES A, B, C
- MATCH 1 AND 2
- FOLD DOWN TAB D AND GLUE TO BACK OF BOB'S HEAD (1)
- FOLD DOWN TAB C AND GLUE TO THE LOWER PART OF 2
- INSERT A PAPER FASTENER THROUGH BOTH HOLES TO ATTACH BOB'S ARM

Now Bob can play!

Ⓐ

Ⓑ

Ⓒ

Ⓓ

① FRONT

② BACK

THE COMPLETED FIGURE SHOULD LOOK LIKE THIS

BOB FOLKROCK 1965

CORDUROY
TROUSERS

CIRCUS
TOP HAT

TRIUMPH
MOTORCYCLES

T-SHIRT
FOR BIKERS!

RAY-BAN
WAYFARER
SUNGLASSES

BLACK LEATHER
JACKET

SHIRT
COLLAR

BEATLE
BOOTS

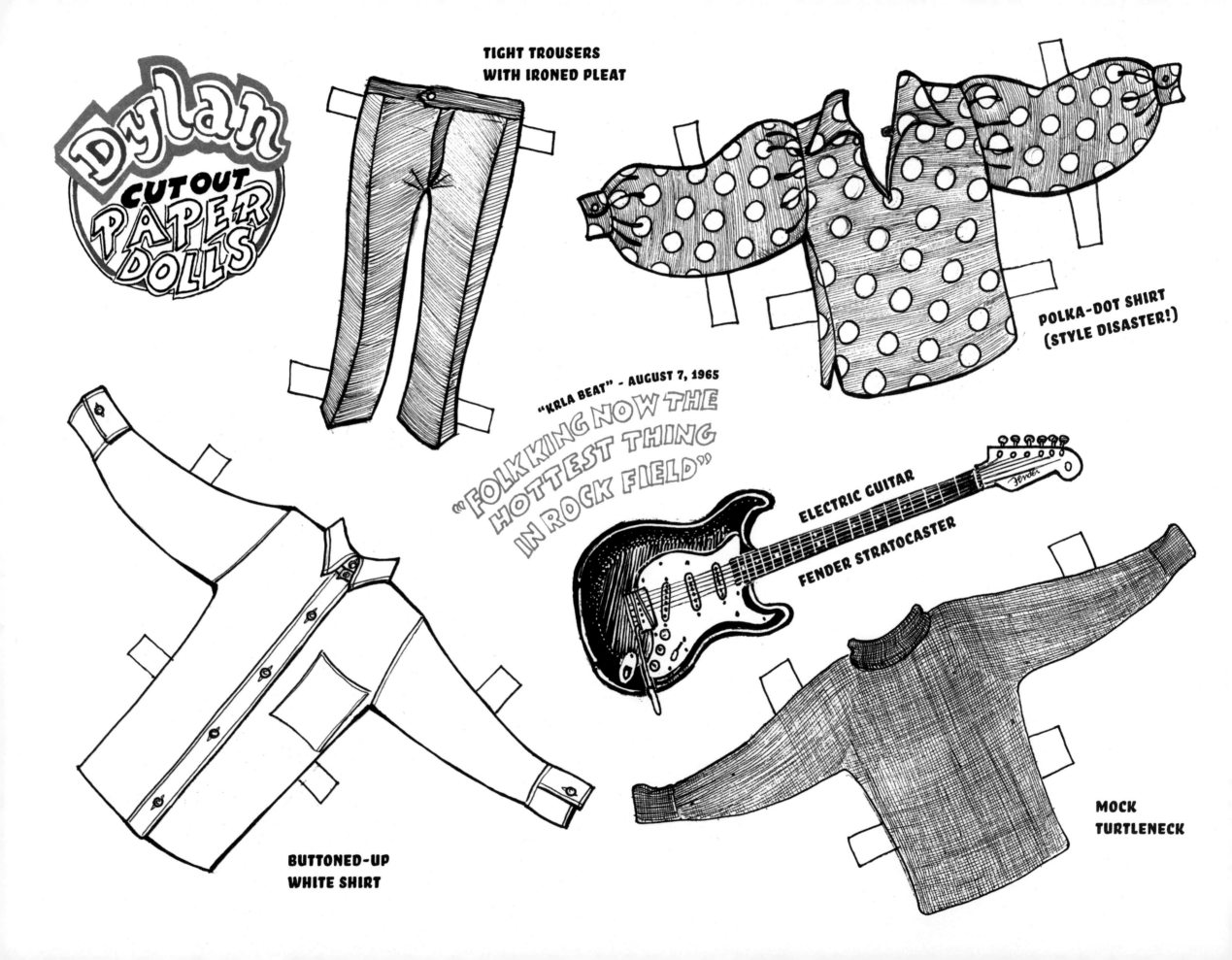

Dylan CUT OUT PAPER DOLLS

TIGHT TROUSERS WITH IRONED PLEAT

POLKA-DOT SHIRT (STYLE DISASTER!)

"KRLA BEAT" – AUGUST 7, 1965

"FOLK KING NOW THE HOTTEST THING IN ROCK FIELD"

ELECTRIC GUITAR

FENDER STRATOCASTER

BUTTONED-UP WHITE SHIRT

MOCK TURTLENECK

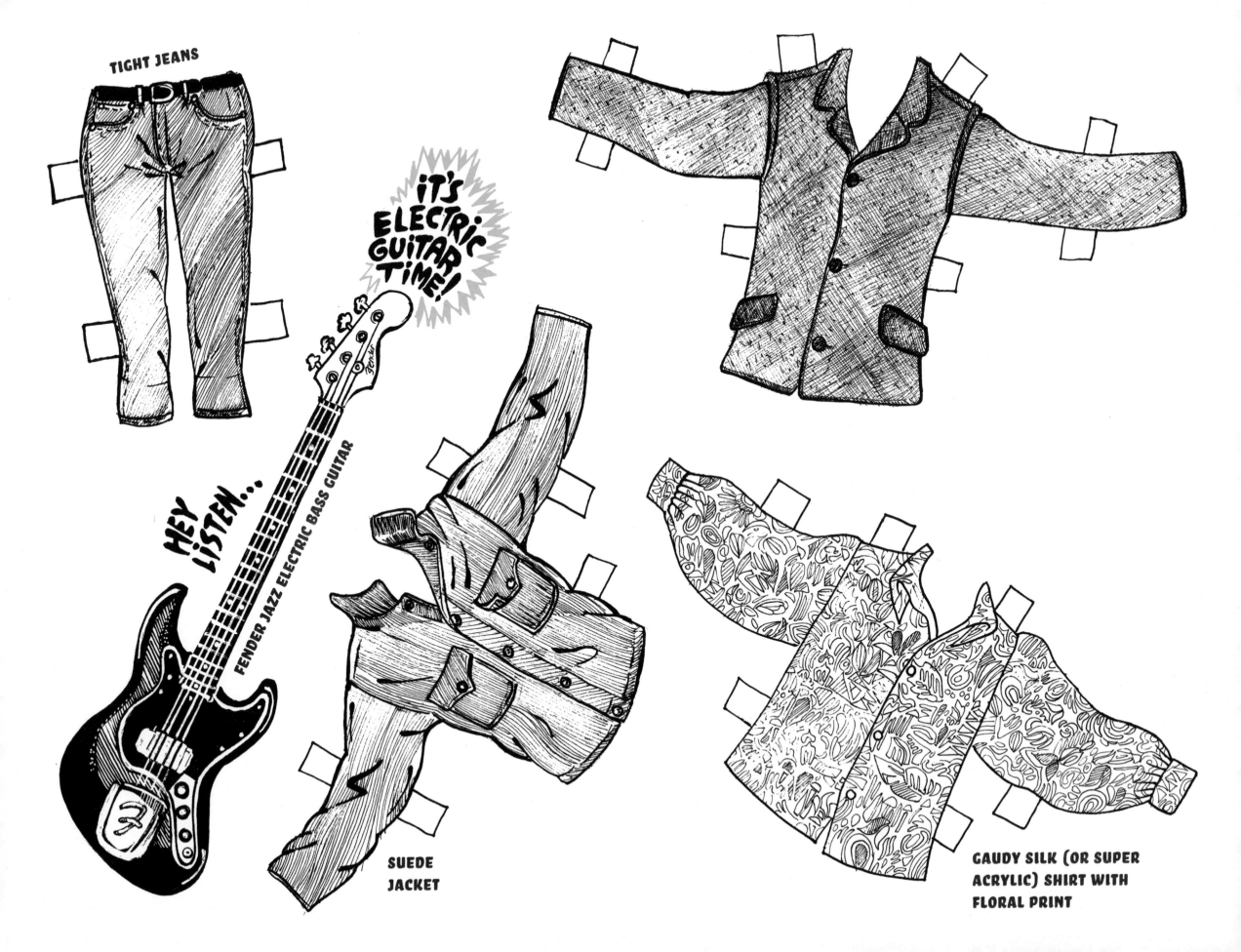

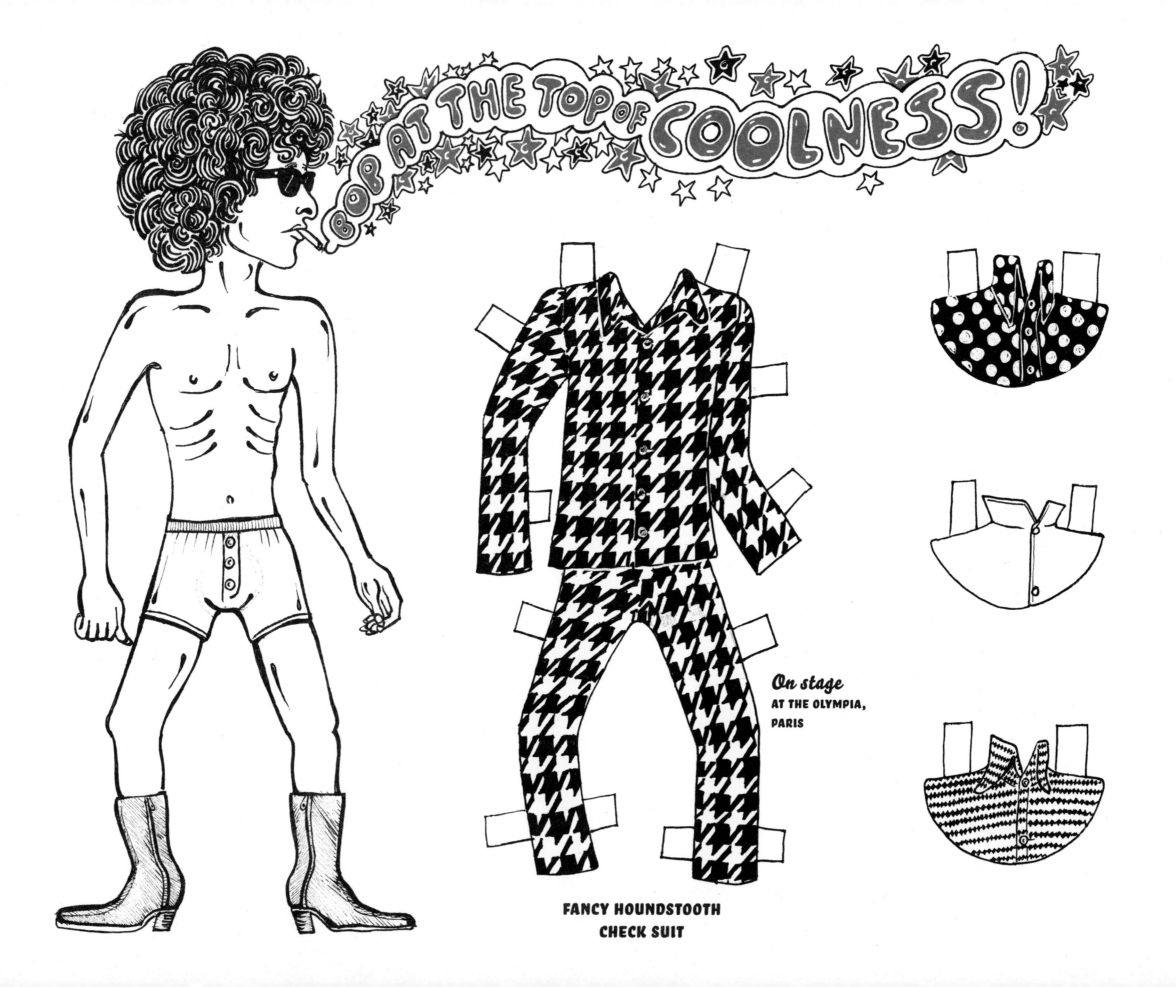

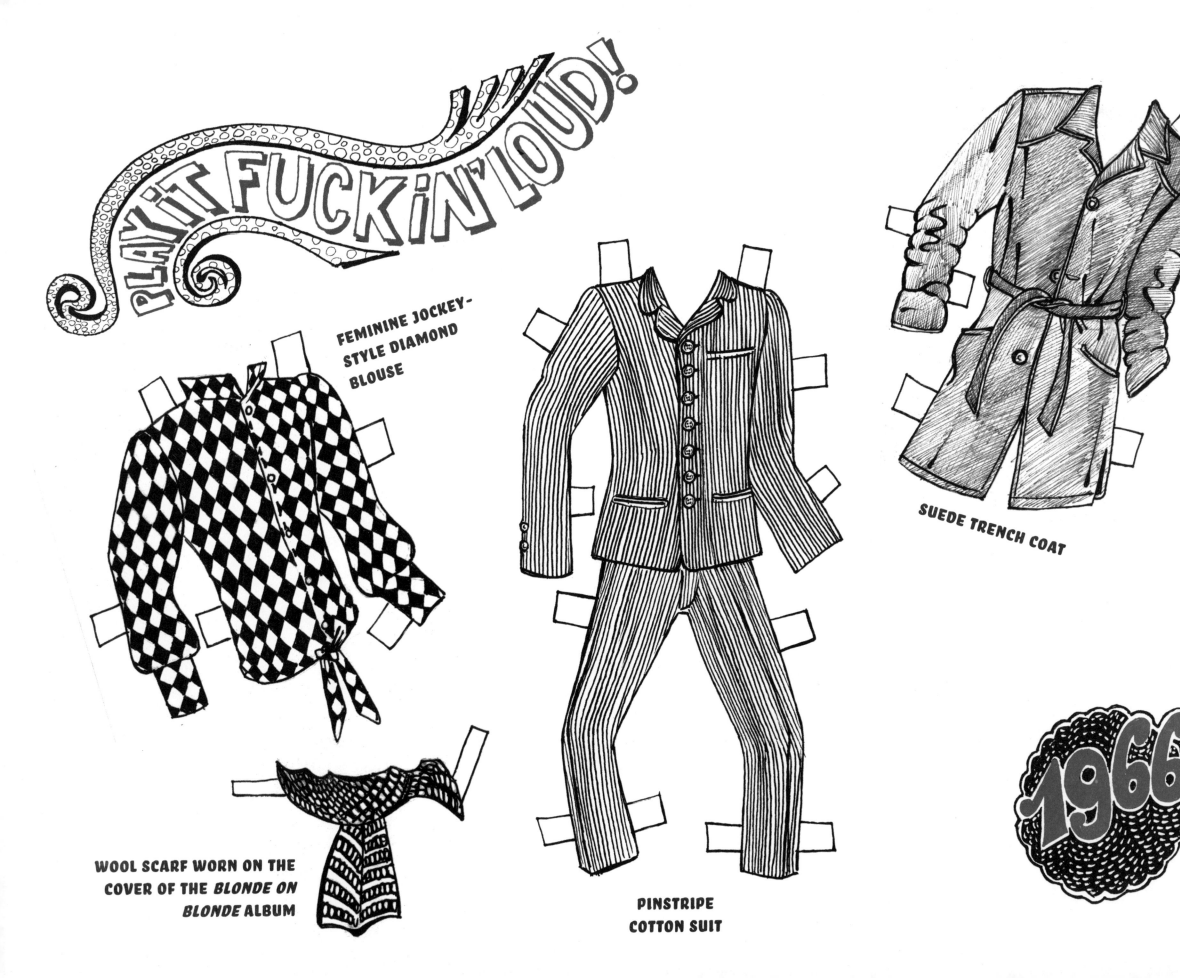

PLAY IT FUCKIN' LOUD!

FEMININE JOCKEY-STYLE DIAMOND BLOUSE

SUEDE TRENCH COAT

WOOL SCARF WORN ON THE COVER OF THE *BLONDE ON BLONDE* ALBUM

PINSTRIPE COTTON SUIT

1966

MILITARY-STYLE SUEDE JACKET

FLORAL OUTFIT WITH CAMOUFLAGE EFFECT

STRIPED SHIRT

STRIPES, STREAKS, LINES EVERYWHERE!

POLKA-DOT SHIRT IN
CLASSIC DYLAN STYLE!

1966

UNLINED STRIPED
COTTON JACKET

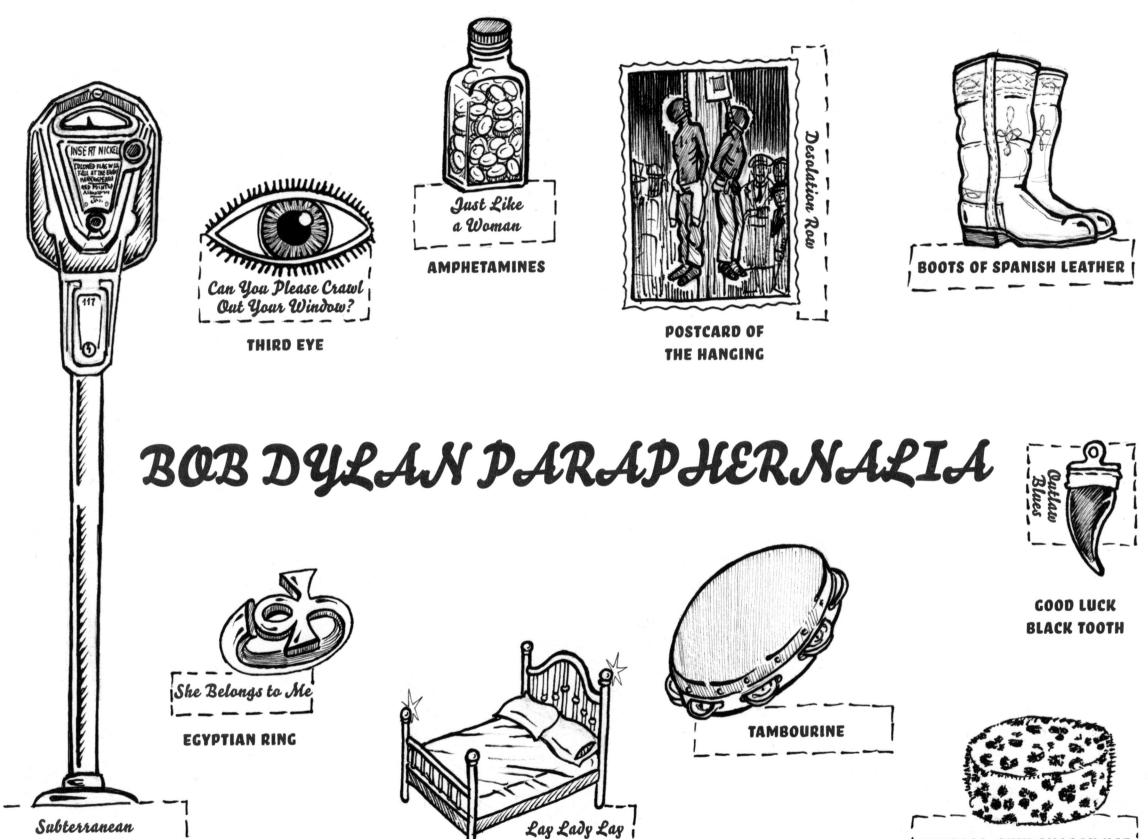

BOB DYLAN PARAPHERNALIA

Subterranean Homesick Blues
PARKING METER

Can You Please Crawl Out Your Window?
THIRD EYE

Just Like a Woman
AMPHETAMINES

Desolation Row
POSTCARD OF THE HANGING

BOOTS OF SPANISH LEATHER

She Belongs to Me
EGYPTIAN RING

Lay Lady Lay
BIG BRASS BED

TAMBOURINE

Outlaw Blues
GOOD LUCK BLACK TOOTH

LEOPARD-SKIN PILLBOX HAT

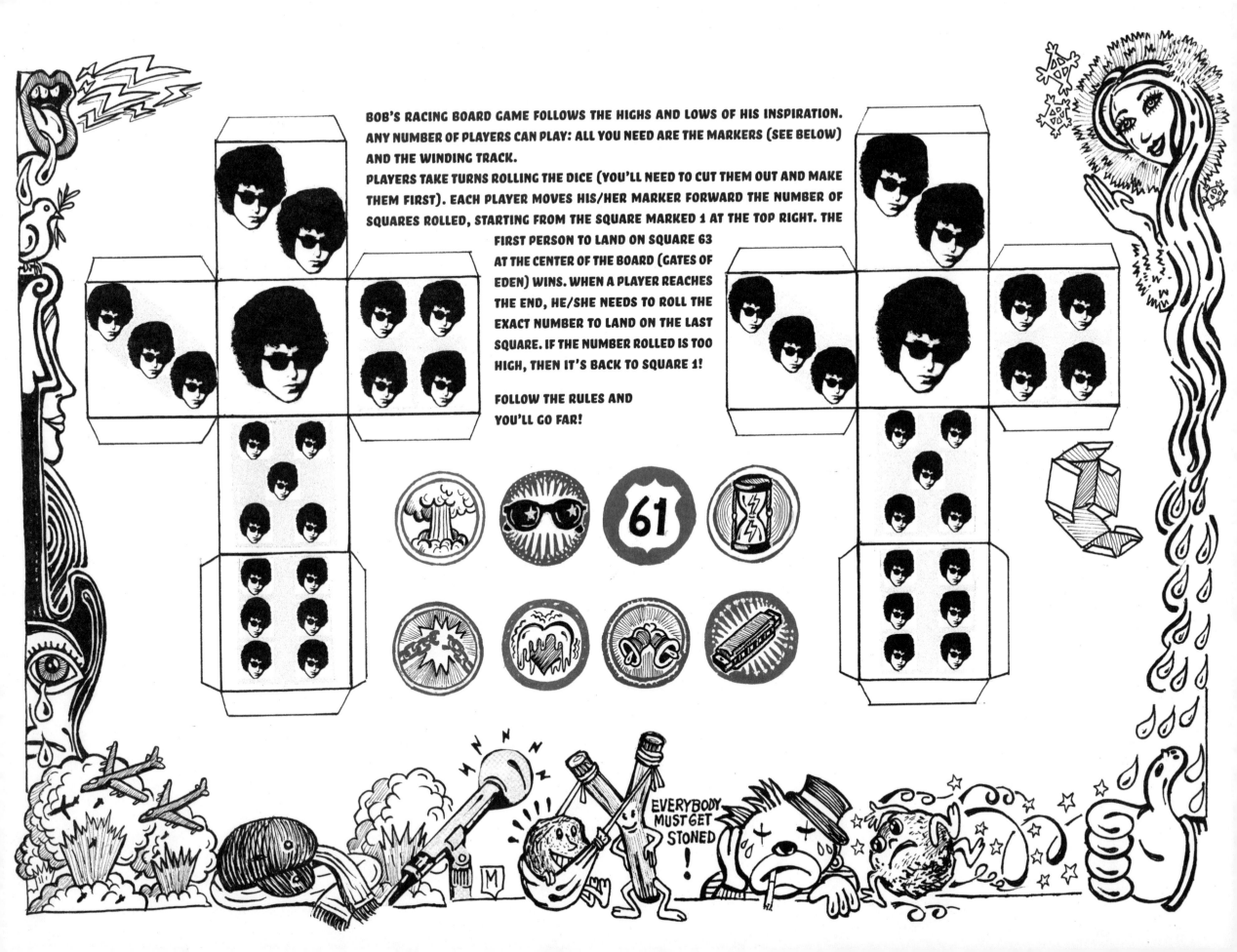

BOB'S RACING BOARD GAME FOLLOWS THE HIGHS AND LOWS OF HIS INSPIRATION. ANY NUMBER OF PLAYERS CAN PLAY: ALL YOU NEED ARE THE MARKERS (SEE BELOW) AND THE WINDING TRACK.
PLAYERS TAKE TURNS ROLLING THE DICE (YOU'LL NEED TO CUT THEM OUT AND MAKE THEM FIRST). EACH PLAYER MOVES HIS/HER MARKER FORWARD THE NUMBER OF SQUARES ROLLED, STARTING FROM THE SQUARE MARKED 1 AT THE TOP RIGHT. THE FIRST PERSON TO LAND ON SQUARE 63 AT THE CENTER OF THE BOARD (GATES OF EDEN) WINS. WHEN A PLAYER REACHES THE END, HE/SHE NEEDS TO ROLL THE EXACT NUMBER TO LAND ON THE LAST SQUARE. IF THE NUMBER ROLLED IS TOO HIGH, THEN IT'S BACK TO SQUARE 1!

FOLLOW THE RULES AND YOU'LL GO FAR!

EVERYBODY MUST GET STONED!

Bob Dylan Circus

I Want You
DANCING CHILD WITH
HIS CHINESE SUIT

Ballad of a Thin Man
SWORD SWALLOWER

Desolation Row
EINSTEIN DISGUISED AS ROBIN HOOD

Girl From the
North Country

GAMES★STORIES★PAPER DOLLS

Love Minus Zero / No Limit
LOVE MINUS ZERO

Ballad of a Thin Man
ONE-EYED MIDGET

Blowin' in the Wind
MOUNTAIN WASHED OUT TO THE SEA

Absolutely Sweet Mary
PERSIAN DRUNKARD

Desolation Row
RESTLESS RIOT SQUAD

Bob Dylan Circus

Magic Box

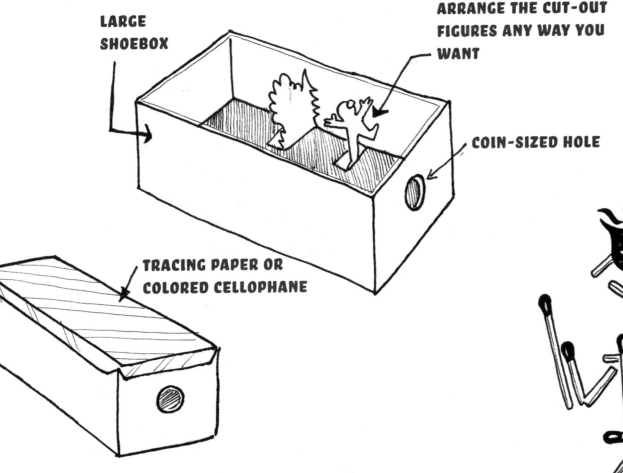

LARGE SHOEBOX

ARRANGE THE CUT-OUT FIGURES ANY WAY YOU WANT

COIN-SIZED HOLE

TRACING PAPER OR COLORED CELLOPHANE

A Hard Rain's A-Gonna Fall
SAD FOREST

How to Build a Magic Box

YOU'LL NEED A LARGE SHOEBOX.

CUT OUT A HOLE THE SIZE OF A LARGE COIN ON ONE OF THE SHORTER SIDES OF THE BOX.

AFTER COLORING IN BOB'S CHARACTERS (OPTIONAL) PLACE THEM INSIDE YOUR MAGIC BOX (THIS IS THE MOST FUN PART). BE SURE TO PLACE THE LARGER FIGURES IN THE BACK AND THE SMALLER ONES IN THE FRONT, AND DON'T PUT TOO MANY FIGURES IN THE BOX AT ONE TIME. LOOK THROUGH THE HOLE TO MAKE SURE NONE OF THE FIGURES COVER UP ANY OF THE OTHERS. YOU SHOULD BE ABLE TO SEE ALL OF THEM. AFTER YOU'VE GLUED EACH ONE FIRMLY IN PLACE, COVER THE TOP OF THE BOX WITH A CLEAN SHEET OF TRACING PAPER. GLUE THE EDGES OF THE PAPER ALONG THE SIDES OF THE BOX. THE ONLY WAY TO SEE WHAT'S INSIDE IS TO PEEP THROUGH THE HOLE... (THE BOX WORKS BEST IN A WELL-LIT PLACE.)

Love Minus Zero/No Limit
STATUE MADE OF MATCH STICKS

Rainy Day Women #12&35
STONED

Gates of Eden
MOTORCYCLE BLACK MADONNA
TWO-WHEELED GYPSY QUEEN

Visions of Johanna
MONA LISA

I GOT THE H'WAY BLUES

I Shall Be Free
DINOSAUR-CATCHER

Desolation Row
OPHELIA

Spanish Harlem Incident
GYPSY GAL

My favorite Bob Dylan songs

1 _____

2 _____

3 _____

4 _____

5 _____

6 _____

7 _____

8 _____

9 _____

10 _____

Draw your own Bob Dylan